FANTASTIC SCIENCE JOURNEYS

A TRIP TO THE SUN

BY CLAIRE FLYNN

Gareth Stevens PUBLISHING

Please visit our website, www.garethstevens.com. For a free color catalog of all our high-quality books, call toll free 1-800-542-2595 or fax 1-877-542-2596.

Library of Congress Cataloging-in-Publication Data

Flynn, Claire.
A trip to the sun / by Claire Flynn.
p. cm. — (Fantastic science journeys)
Includes index.
ISBN 978-1-4824-2014-2 (pbk.)
ISBN 978-1-4824-2013-5 (6-pack)
ISBN 978-1-4824-2015-9 (library binding)
1. Sun — Juvenile literature. I. Flynn, Claire E. II. Title.
QB521.5 F59 2015
523.7—d23

Published in 2015 by
Gareth Stevens Publishing
111 East 14th Street, Suite 349
New York, NY 10003

Designer: Sarah Liddell
Editor: Ryan Nagelhout

Photo credits: Cover, p. 1 silver tiger/Shutterstock.com; p. 5 Pakhnyushcha/Shutterstock.com; pp. 7, 27 Vladimir Arndt/Shutterstock.com; pp. 9, 25 Triff/Shutterstock.com; p. 11 Alin Brotea/Shutterstock.com; p. 13 (main and inset) photo courtesy of NASA/SDO; p. 15 photo courtesy of NASA; p. 17 Mopic/Shutterstock.com; p. 19 Mike Agliolo/Getty Images; p. 21 (main) VICTOR HABBICK VISIONS/Getty Images; p. 21 (northern lights) Corepics VOF/Shutterstock.com; p. 23 fluidworkshop/Shutterstock.com; p. 29 (main) tr3gin/Shutterstock.com; p. 29 (solar eclipse) Juergen Faelchle/Shutterstock.com.

Printed in the United States of America

CPSIA compliance information: Batch #CW15GS: For further information contact Gareth Stevens, New York, New York at 1-800-542-2595.

CONTENTS

Let's Hop into a Spacecraft! 4
Miles and Miles. 6
The Sun Was Born!. 8
Feeling Hot, Hot, Hot! 12
The Sun's Six Layers. 14
Convection 16
Solar Winds 18
The Best Light Show in the Universe!. . . . 20
Exploring Our Solar System 22
The Sun's Role in Our Weather 24
Ready to Blow? 26
We Can't Live Without It! 28
Glossary. 30
For More Information. 31
Index 32

Words in the glossary appear in **bold** type the first time they are used in the text.

LET'S HOP INTO A SPACECRAFT!

The sun is so amazing! Have you ever looked up at the sky and wanted to learn more about that glowing ball? Can you imagine getting into a special spacecraft that would let you safely travel to the sun?

Hope you brought your sunglasses, because that's exactly what we're going to do. Let's hop into our ship and blast off so we can take a closer look at the sun and what makes it so amazing!

THAT'S FANTASTIC!

Never look directly at the sun because you could hurt your eyes. **Astronomers** use special telescopes that allow them to safely take a closer look.

The sun is at the
center of our solar system.

MILES AND MILES

It's a good thing our spacecraft is superfast, because the sun's about 93 million miles (150 million km) from Earth. If we could hop into a car and drive to the sun at 70 miles (113 km) per hour, it would take us about 152 years to get there!

Once we reach the sun, it's hard to imagine just how big it is. Over 1 million Earths could fit inside it! The **circumference** of the sun is a whopping 2.7 million miles (4.4 million km).

THAT'S FANTASTIC!

It takes about 8 minutes for the sun's light to reach Earth.

The sun's light and warmth are what allow life on Earth to exist.

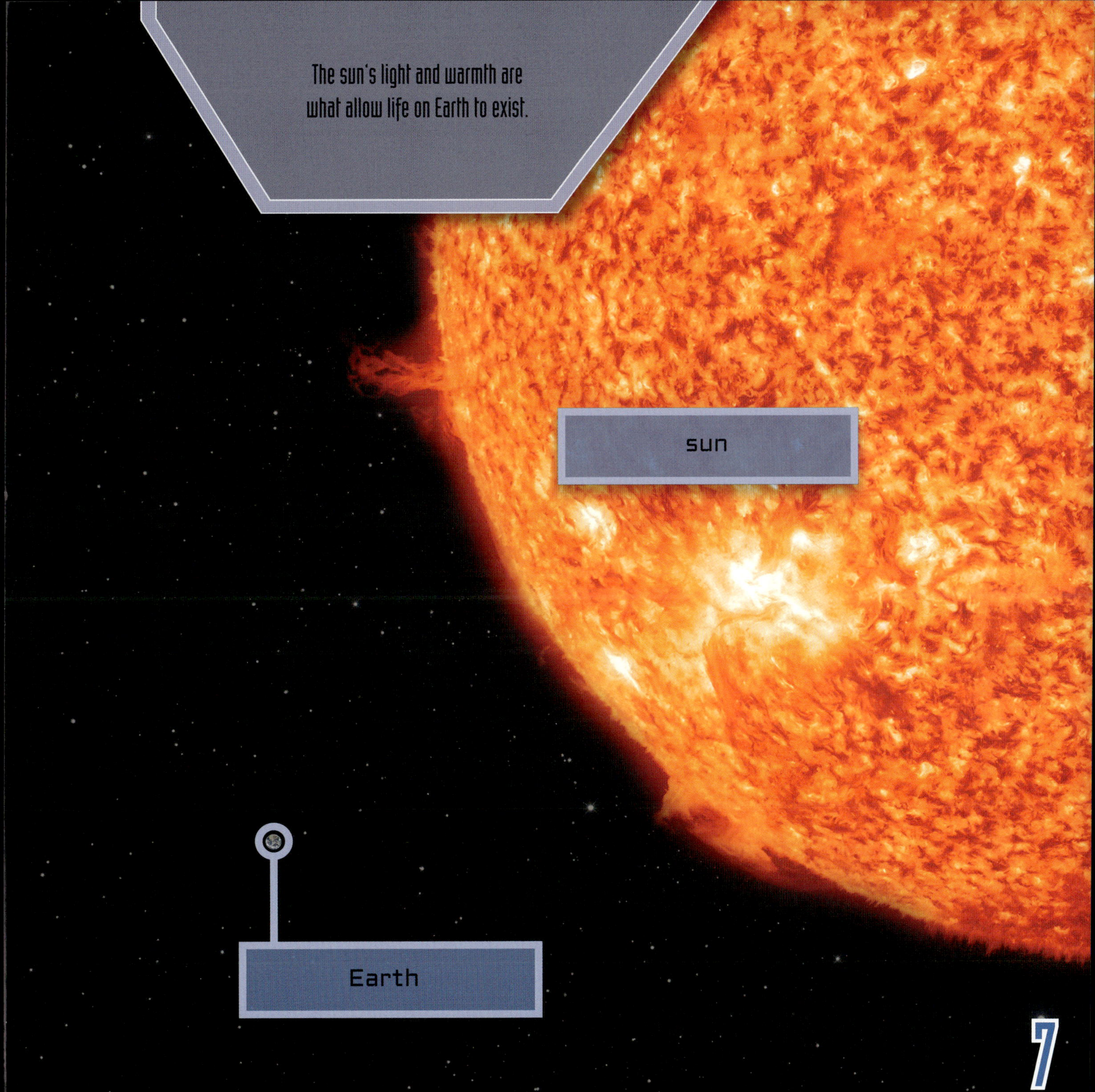

THE SUN WAS BORN!

The sun was created about 4.5 billion years ago. It's not a planet, but a star. Stars are really big balls of gas. The sun is made of about 92 percent hydrogen and 8 percent helium.

There are stars much larger than the sun, but the sun is the closest star to Earth, so it looks bigger. From Earth, the other billions of stars look like tiny dots of light.

THAT'S FANTASTIC!

There are more stars in the universe than there are grains of sand on Earth!

Because of its color and size, the sun is considered a yellow dwarf star.

The sun started out much smaller than it is today. Billions of years ago, a cloud of gases and dust came together under the force of **gravity**. The pressure and heat increased, and the ball grew hotter and hotter. It became so hot that its core **ignited**, causing nuclear fusion.

Nuclear fusion is the process by which stars produce their own energy. Stars change hydrogen into helium and give off energy in the process.

THAT'S FANTASTIC!

The word "helium" comes from the name of the ancient Greek god of the sun, Helios.

By using telescopes, we can see new stars being born far away from Earth.

FEELING HOT, HOT, HOT!

As our ship gets closer to the sun, we start to feel just how hot it is. The surface of the sun is about 10,000°F (5,538°C)! If that's too hot for you, we'll find some sunspots. These parts appear darker on images taken by astronomers because they're actually cooler than other parts of the sun.

If we were to reach the sun's core, it would get even hotter! The core reaches more than 27,000,000°F (115,000,000°C), but for now let's land on the surface of the sun.

THAT'S FANTASTIC!

Sunspots don't always exist in the same place. Even the number of sunspots on our sun can change.

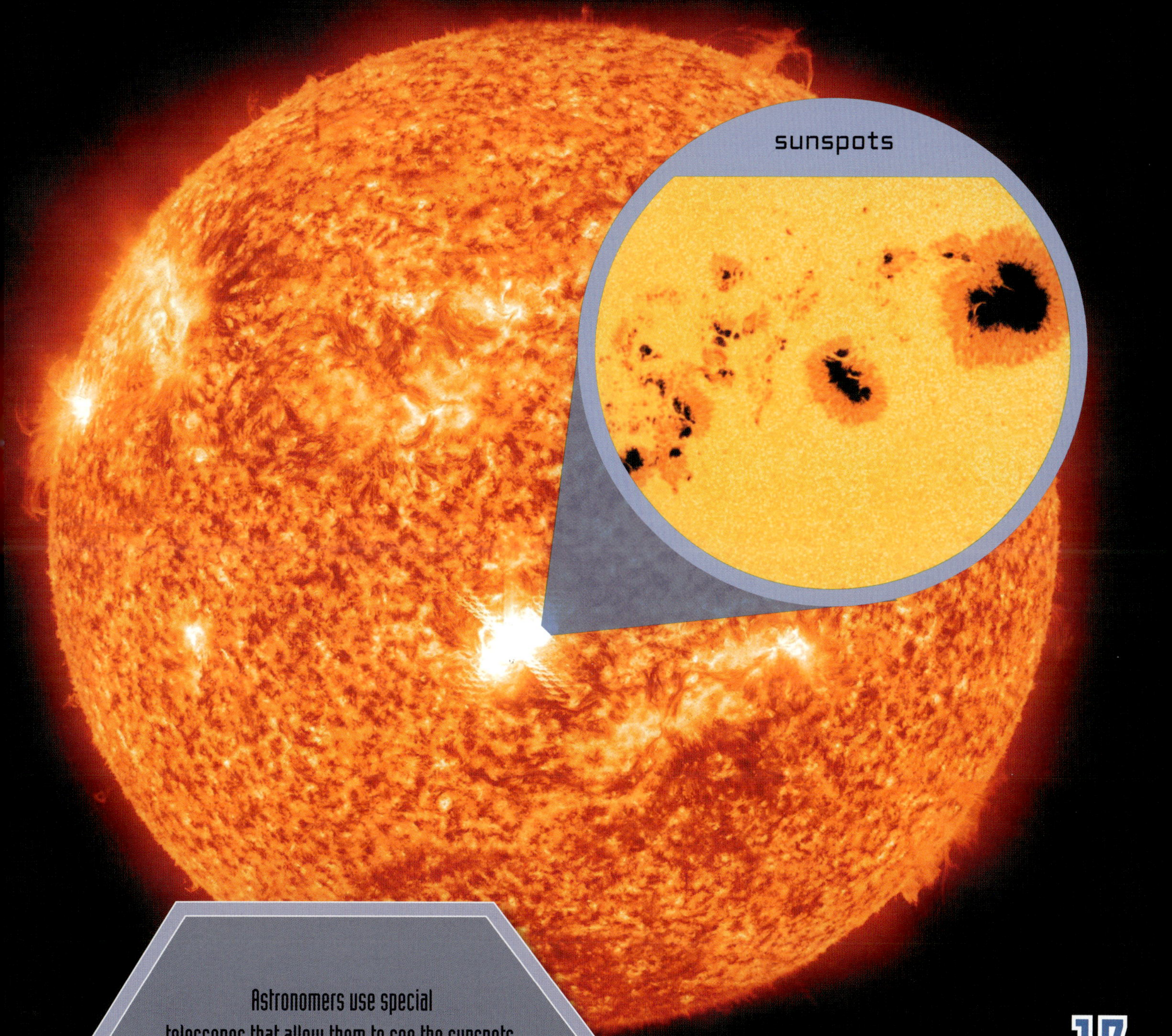

Astronomers use special telescopes that allow them to see the sunspots.

THE SUN'S SIX LAYERS

We know the center of the sun, its core, is the hottest part. It also produces all the sun's energy. The next layer is called the **radiative** zone. This carries energy out from the core to the convective zone. Next comes the atmosphere of the sun, starting with the photosphere, where the light we see from the sun comes from.

The fifth layer is the chromosphere, which is filled with hydrogen. The outermost layer of the sun is the corona, which is a cloud of gas and **plasma**.

THAT'S FANTASTIC!

It takes more than a million years for the energy from the core to reach the surface of the sun.

LAYERS OF THE SUN

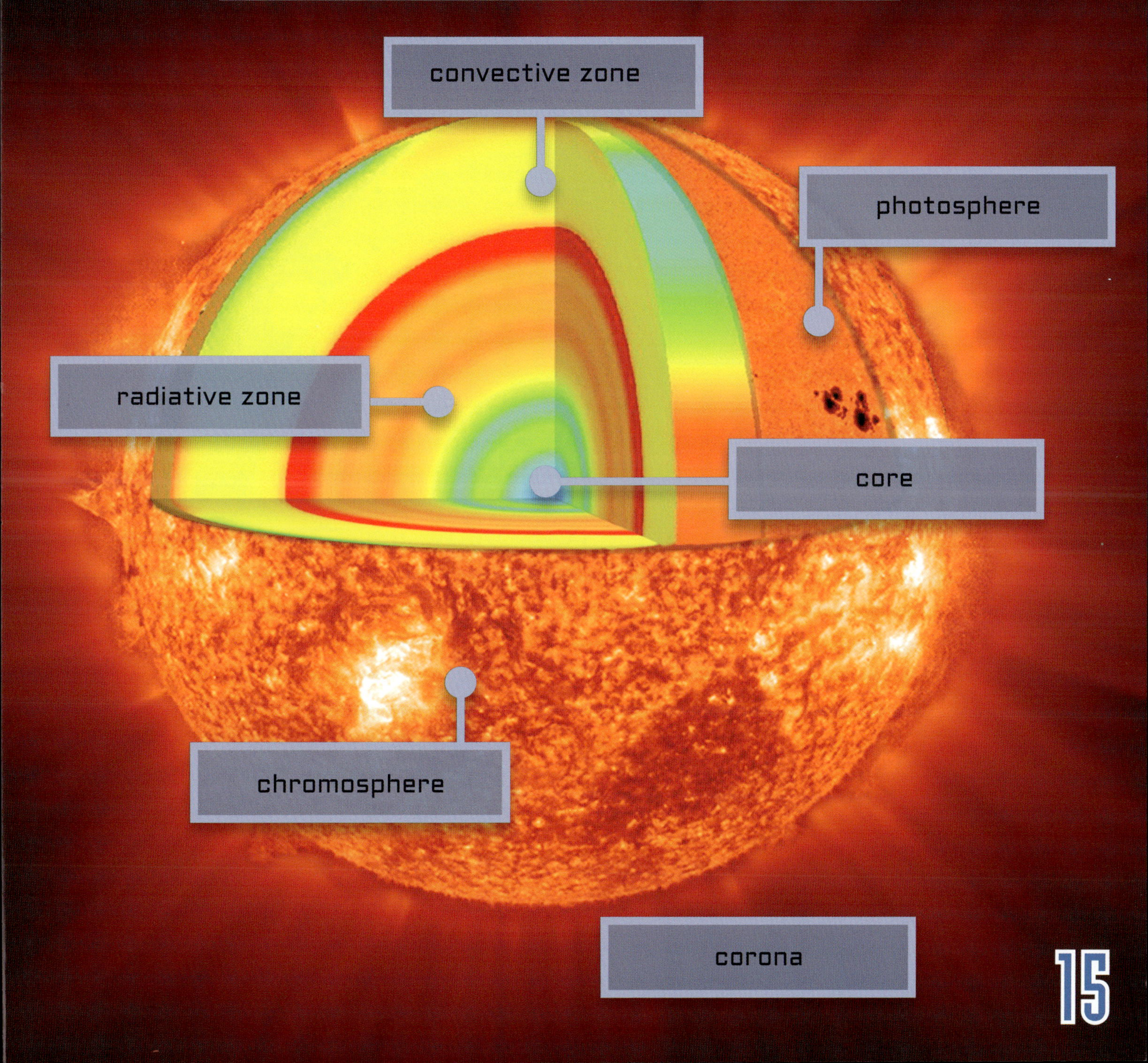

CONVECTION

As our ship travels through the layers of the sun you'll probably notice the temperatures are ever changing. This is due to something called convection. Have you ever noticed an attic is often hot, while basements stay cool? This is because warm air rises while cool air falls. The same thing happens in the sun!

As the gases in the core are heated, they rise, while the cooler gases sink back into the core. This constant circle of gas within stars is called convection.

THAT'S FANTASTIC!

A single atom may rise and fall for millions of years before it reaches the surface.

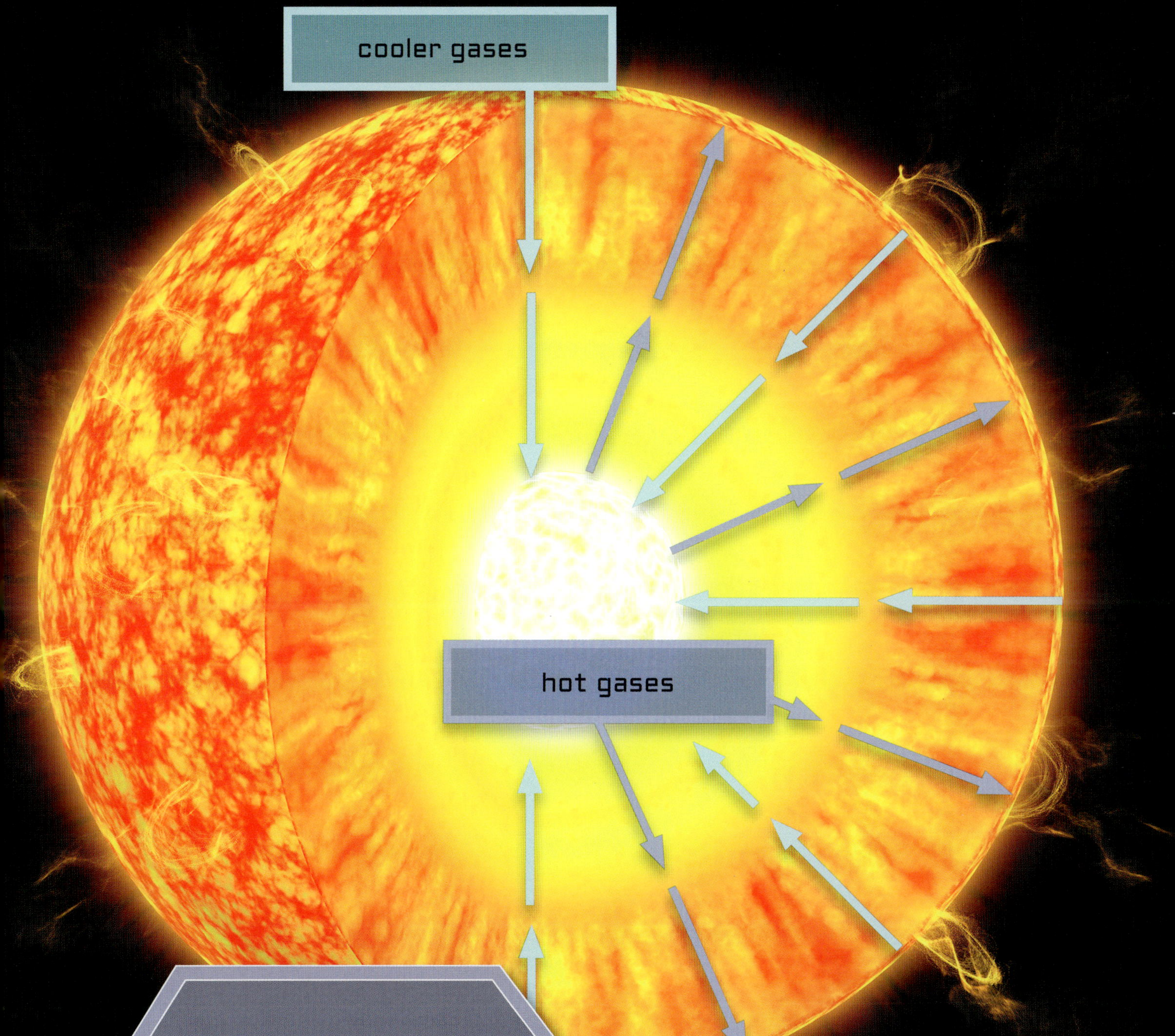

Because of convection, temperatures inside the sun are always changing.

SOLAR WINDS

It's feeling a bit breezy on the sun! As the sun's core turns hydrogen into helium, it lets tiny bits of particles—or atoms—out into space. The sun's radiation and these atoms make a type of wind known as solar wind.

The atoms are released away from the sun in all directions. Right at this very moment, atoms are traveling our way. The solar wind created by the sun also mixes with other stars' wind.

THAT'S FANTASTIC!

The atoms released from the sun travel right through our bodies without us even knowing!

An atom is the smallest bit of an element that can exist alone in the universe.

THE BEST LIGHT SHOW IN THE UNIVERSE!

Back down on Earth, the solar wind can sometimes be seen as what we call the northern and the southern lights. People in some parts of the world can look into the sky and see a beautiful light show!

The northern and the southern lights are caused by solar flares, which happen when the sun releases a huge amount of gases and plasma into space. When they reach Earth's atmosphere, the skies light up at night! In the Northern **Hemisphere**, these lights are referred to as the aurora borealis.

THAT'S FANTASTIC!

There are actual hotels and glass igloos people can stay in to view the northern lights in countries far north, such as Finland.

The scientific name for the southern lights is aurora australis.

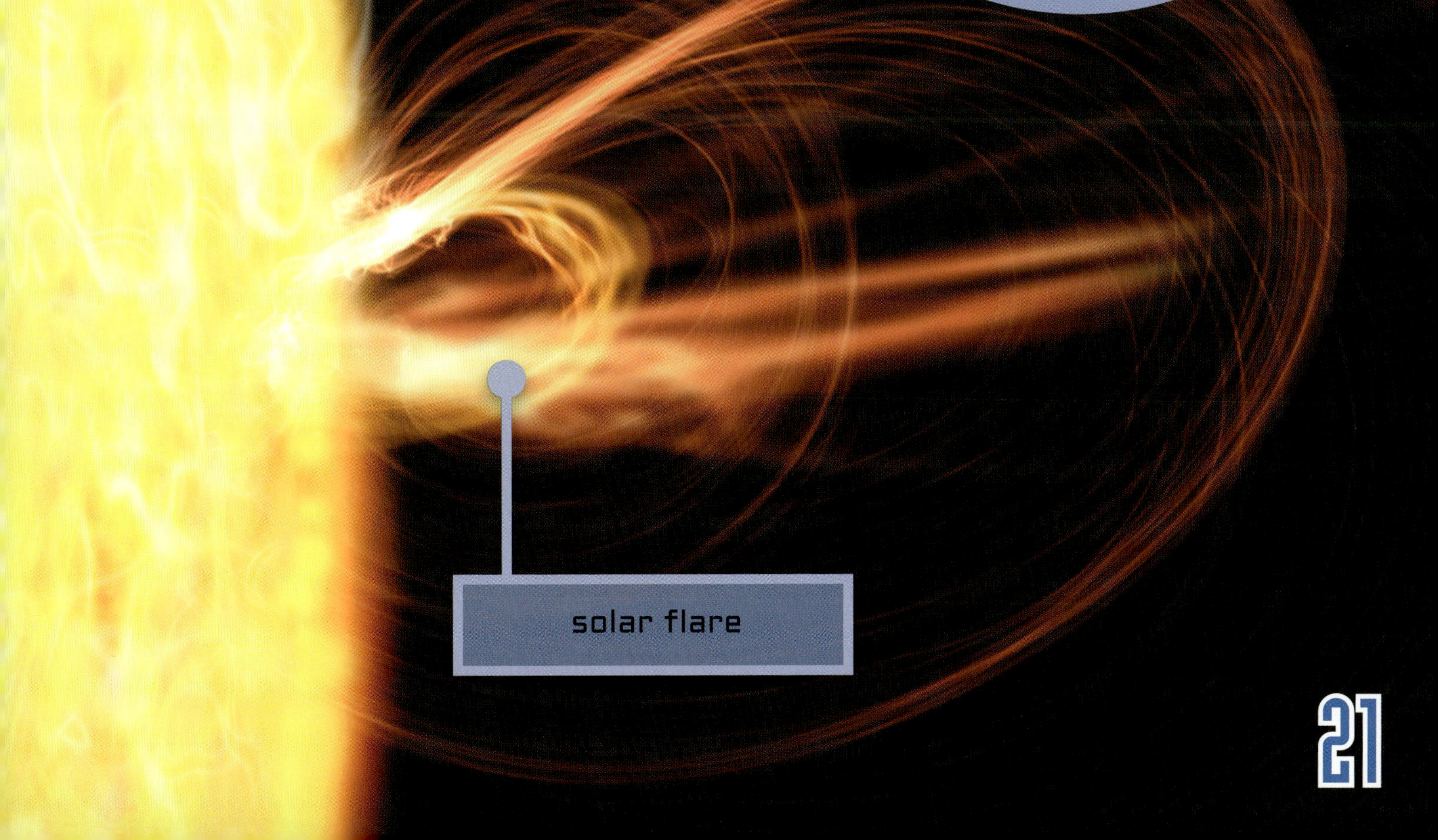

EXPLORING OUR SOLAR SYSTEM

Now that we know how the sun works, let's fly our ship to the rest of the solar system. Everything in the solar system orbits, or travels in a circle around, the sun because of its gravitational pull.

There are eight planets in the solar system, but the sun contains 99.86 percent of the solar system's mass. The sun is also the only object in the solar system that makes its own light. Everything else reflects, or throws back, the sun's light.

THAT'S FANTASTIC!

There were nine planets in our solar system until Pluto was **reclassified** as a dwarf planet in 2006.

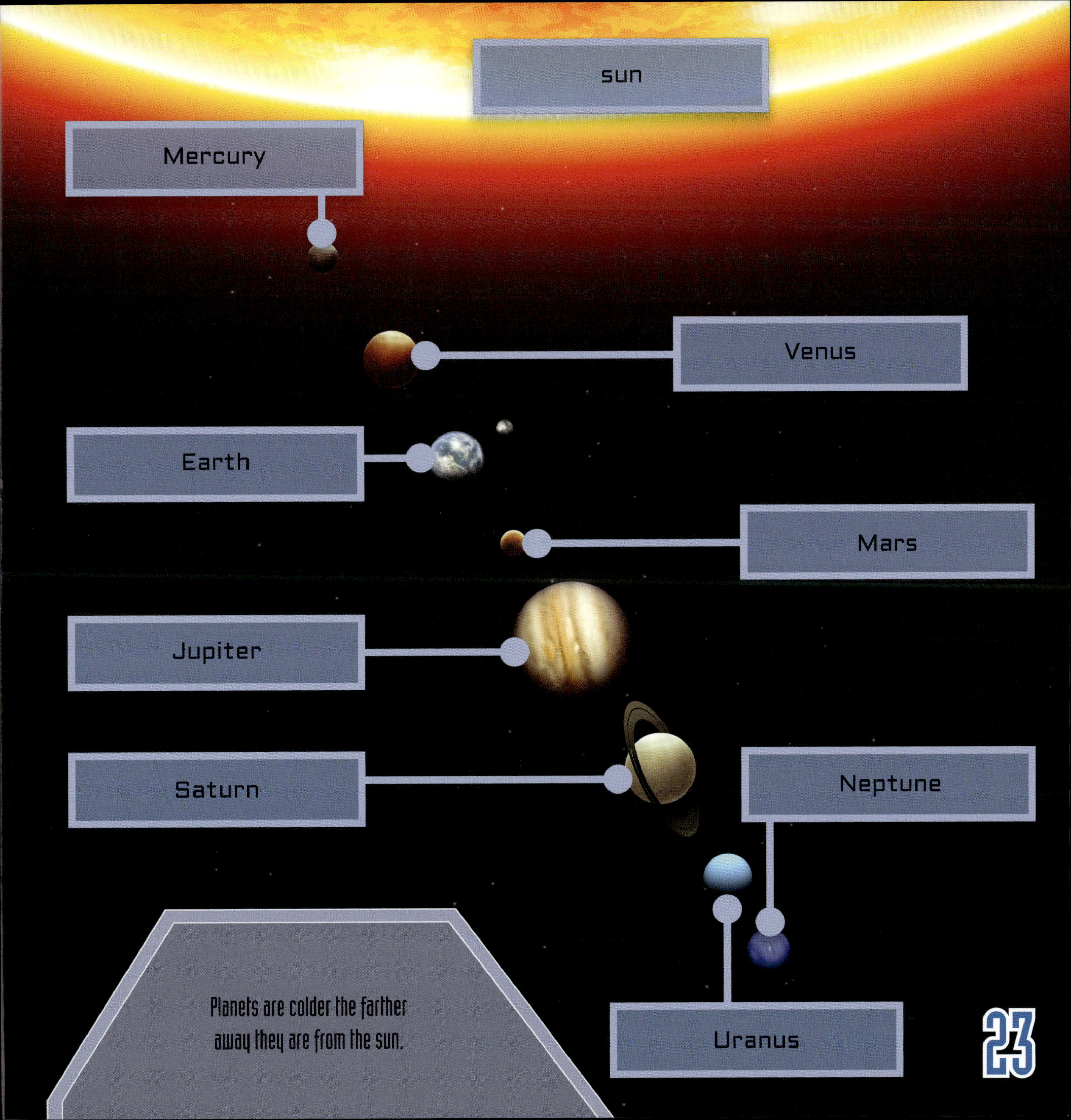

Planets are colder the farther away they are from the sun.

THE SUN'S ROLE IN OUR WEATHER

All that energy coming from the sun helps create our weather on Earth. Since Earth is almost round, the sun's rays reach different parts of it at different times and angles. Temperatures are usually warmer near the **equator** because it gets more direct sun. Temperatures are milder away from the equator and get very cold near the poles.

Earth's orbit also causes seasonal changes: winter, spring, summer, and fall. Places having winter see colder weather, while summer weather is warmer.

THAT'S FANTASTIC!

Even the wind on Earth is caused by the sun! Air warmed by the sun rises, and cool air moves in below it.

Different weather and temperatures exist on Earth because differerent amounts of the sun's energy reach the planet's surface.

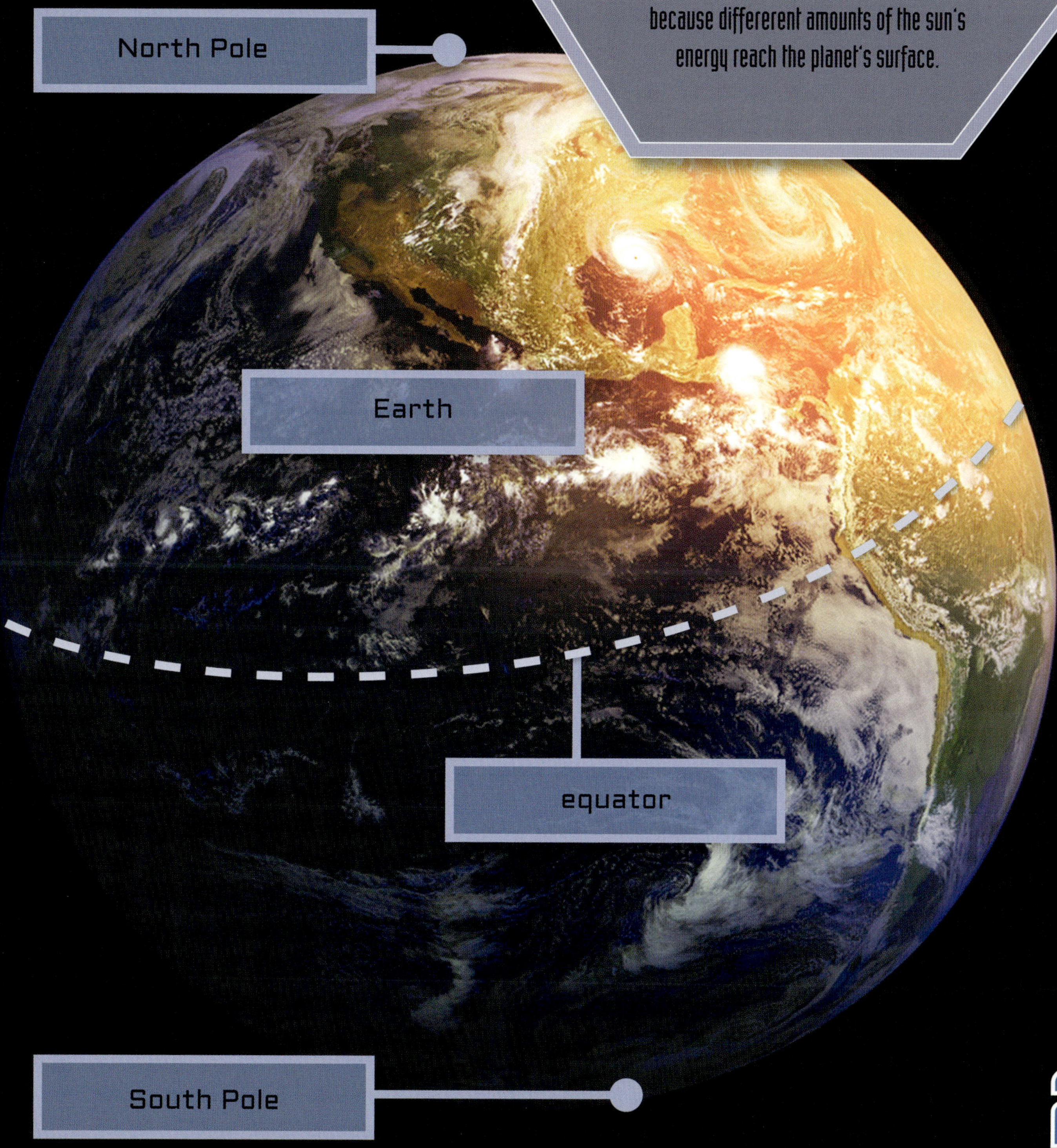

READY TO BLOW?

We know the sun uses hydrogen for fuel. But what happens if the sun runs out of hydrogen? Well, when stars run out of fuel, they start to change! Yellow dwarf stars start to get bigger and turn orange, then they grow even larger and become red giant stars.

Red giant stars send out about 1,000 times more energy than our current sun, which would bake Earth and might blow away our atmosphere. Thankfully, scientists say the sun has about 5 billion years of hydrogen fuel left.

THAT'S FANTASTIC!

Thanks to the telescope in our ship, we can see what happens to planets orbiting nearby stars when they change. We see the broken pieces of a small planet that once orbited a red giant about 170 **light-years** from Earth.

Supermassive stars explode when they run out of hydrogen fuel, but scientists don't think our sun will create that kind of **supernova**.

WE CAN'T LIVE WITHOUT IT!

Now that we've learned about the sun and its role in our solar system, it's time to get back to Earth and cool off. What an amazing journey we took in our special ship!

We now know that without the light and energy from the sun, all life on Earth would perish. So the next time you look up in the sky, remember how important that yellow ball is! And put on some sunscreen so you don't get burned!

THAT'S FANTASTIC!

A solar eclipse happens when the moon passes between the sun and Earth. Only the sun's chromosphere and corona are visible. Special eye protection must be worn to see this safely.

Even without a trip to space, people throughout history have understood how important the sun is to life on Earth.

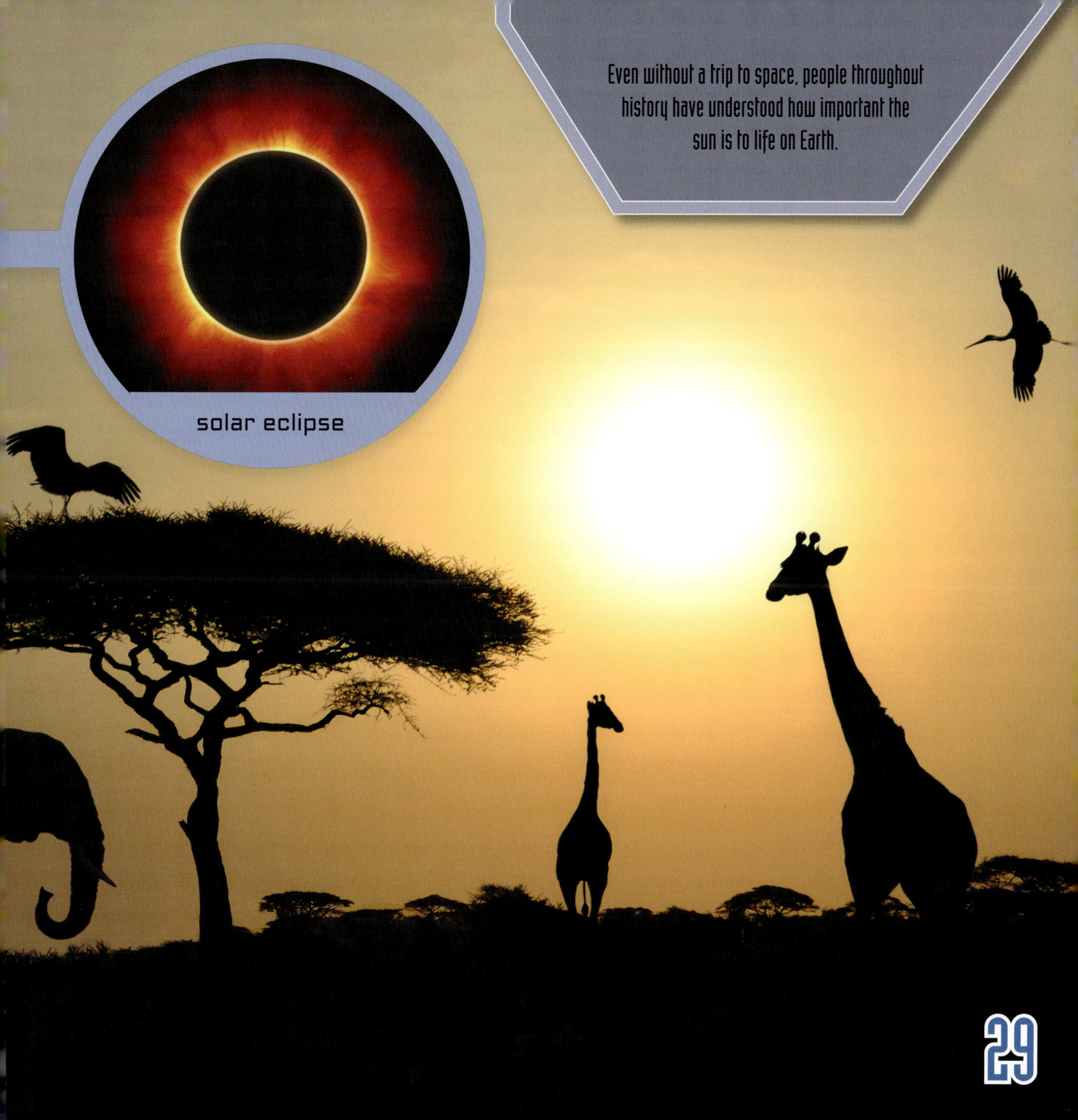

solar eclipse

GLOSSARY

astronomer: a person who studies stars and planets

circumference: the distance around a ball-shaped object at its widest point

equator: an imaginary line around Earth the same distance from the North and South Poles

gravity: the force that pulls objects toward the center of a planet or star

hemisphere: one half of Earth

ignite: to catch fire

light-year: the distance light can travel in a year

plasma: a hot gas made up of parts of atoms that carry an electric charge

radiative: having to do with the process of sending out

reclassify: to put something in a new class or category

supernova: the explosion of a very large star

FOR MORE INFORMATION

BOOKS

Graham, Ian. *Our Sun*. Mankato, MN: Smart Apple Media, 2015.

Heos, Bridget. *What Is the Sun?* New York, NY: Rosen Publishing, 2015.

Riggs, Kate. *The Sun*. Mankato, MN: Creative Education, 2015.

WEBSITES

Astronomy for Kids: Sun
kidsastronomy.com/our_sun.htm
Find out more about how the sun works on this site.

Planets for Kids: Sun
planetsforkids.org/star-sun.html
Find fun facts and more about our solar system's sun here.

Sun Facts for Kids
sciencekids.co.nz/sciencefacts/space/sun.html
Learn more great facts about our sun.

Publisher's note to educators and parents: Our editors have carefully reviewed these websites to ensure that they are suitable for students. Many websites change frequently, however, and we cannot guarantee that a site's future contents will continue to meet our high standards of quality and educational value. Be advised that students should be closely supervised whenever they access the Internet.

INDEX

atoms 16, 18, 19
chromosphere 14, 28
convection 16, 17
convective zone 14
core 12, 14, 16
corona 14, 28
Earth 6, 8, 11, 20, 24, 26, 28, 29
energy 10, 14, 24, 25, 26, 28
equator 24
gases 8, 10, 14, 16, 20
helium 10, 18
hydrogen 10, 14, 18, 26, 27
light 6, 7, 14, 20, 22, 28
northern lights 20
nuclear fusion 10
photosphere 14
planet 8, 22, 23, 25, 26
plasma 14, 20
poles 24
radiative zone 14
red giant stars 26
solar eclipse 28
solar flares 20
solar system 5, 22, 28
solar wind 18, 20
southern lights 20, 21
stars 8, 9, 10, 11, 26
sunspots 12, 13
supernova 27
weather 24, 25
yellow dwarf star 9, 26